Dear Parent:

Congratulations! Your child is taking the first steps on an exciting journey. The destination? Independent reading!

STEP INTO READING® will help your child get there. The program offers five steps to reading success. Each step includes fun stories and colorful art. There are also Step into Reading Sticker Books, Step into Reading Math Readers, Step into Reading Write-In Readers, Step into Reading Phonics Readers, and Step into Reading Phonics First Steps! Boxed Sets—a complete literacy program with something for every child.

Learning to Read, Step by Step!

Ready to Read Preschool–Kindergarten
• big type and easy words • rhyme and rhythm • picture clues
For children who know the alphabet and are eager to begin reading.

Reading with Help   Preschool–Grade 1
• basic vocabulary • short sentences • simple stories
For children who recognize familiar words and sound out new words with help.

Reading on Your Own Grades 1–3
• engaging characters • easy-to-follow plots • popular topics
For children who are ready to read on their own.

Reading Paragraphs Grades 2–3
• challenging vocabulary • short paragraphs • exciting stories
For newly independent readers who read simple sentences with confidence.

Ready for Chapters Grades 2–4
• chapters • longer paragraphs • full-color art
For children who want to take the plunge into chapter books but still like colorful pictures.

STEP INTO READING® is designed to give every child a successful reading experience. The grade levels are only guides. Children can progress through the steps at their own speed, developing confidence in their reading, no matter what their grade.

Remember, a lifetime love of reading starts with a single step!

To Murph Shapiro: a man/principal with grace, compassion, and humor.
For the super Team 6-3 at the Oak Hill Middle School. For the "A"
Team: Rochelle Solomon, Chuck Berk, Fred Lown, Amrita Shlachter,
Robert Shlachter, Sandy Siegel, and Joseph Tovares. For my Tali and
Gabe: ". . . more than there are stars in the sky—always."
And for my "out of this world" editors: Suzy Capozzi,
Shana Corey, and Heidi Kilgras—many thanx! —E.A.

For my children, Kristina and Steve. The future is yours: Imagination
has no limits, so you might as well shoot for the stars. —G.T.

Acknowledgments: With special thanks to Stephanie L. Parello, Astronomy Education
Coordinator at the American Museum of Natural History's Hayden Planetarium, for
her time and expertise in reviewing this book.

Photo credits: cover: National Aeronautics and Space Administration (*NASA*); p. 6: © *Space Island Group*; p. 7: Marshall Space Flight Center/*NASA*; p. 9: Johnson Space Center/*NASA*; p. 14: © Danny Lehman/*CORBIS*; p. 15: © Macduff Everton/*CORBIS*; p. 16: (Ptolemy) © Michael Nicholson/*CORBIS*, (Copernicus) © Bettmann/*CORBIS*; p. 17: © Bettmann/*CORBIS*; p. 25: © Bettmann/*CORBIS*; p. 27: © Kennedy Space Center/*NASA*; p. 28: (Gagarin) © Bettmann/*CORBIS*, (Shepard) Johnson Space Center/*NASA*, (Glenn) Marshall Space Flight Center/*NASA*; p. 29: (Tereshkova) © Bettmann/*CORBIS*, (Ride) Johnson Space Center/*NASA*, (Armstrong) Dryden Flight Research Center–USAF/*NASA*, (Bluford) Johnson Space Center/*NASA*; p. 30: (Jemison) Johnson Space Center/*NASA*, (Onizuka) © Michael S. Yamashita/*CORBIS*, (Chang-Diaz) Johnson Space Center/*NASA*, (Ochoa) *NASA*; pp. 36–37: NASA and the Hubble Heritage Team (STScI/AURA) [Acknowledgment: R. G. French (Wellesley College), J. Cuzzi (NASA/Ames), L. Dones (SwRI), and J. Lissauer (NASA/Ames)]/*NASA*; p. 38: NASA/JPL-Caltech/*NASA*; p. 39: Dr. R. Albrecht, ESA/ESO Space Telescope European Coordinating Facility/*NASA*; p. 43: Marshall Space Flight Center/*NASA*; p. 44: Johnson Space Center/*NASA*; p. 45: Goddard Space Flight Center/*NASA*; p. 46: (Cat's Eye Nebula) J. P. Harrington and K. J. Borkowski (University of Maryland)/*NASA*, (Sombrero Nebula) NASA and the Hubble Heritage Team (STScI/AURA)/*NASA*; p. 47: © Reuters/*CORBIS*.

www.stepintoreading.com

Educators and librarians, for a variety of teaching tools, visit us at
www.randomhouse.com/teachers

Library of Congress Cataloging-in-Publication Data
Arnold, Eric.
Race into space / by Eric Arnold ; illustrated by Gary Torrisi. — 1st ed.
   p. cm. — (Step into reading)
ISBN 0-375-80195-2 (trade) — ISBN 0-375-90195-7 (lib. bdg.)
1. Outer space—Exploration—Juvenile literature. 2. Space stations—Juvenile literature.
I. Torrisi, Gary, ill. II. Title. III. Series.
TL793.A764 2004 919.904—dc22 2004009257

RACE INTO SPACE

by Eric Arnold
illustrated by Gary Torrisi

Random House 🏠 New York

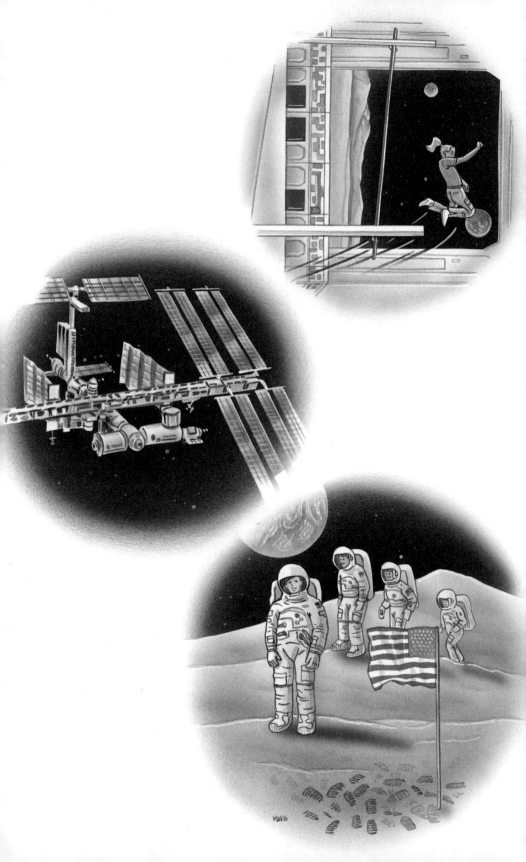

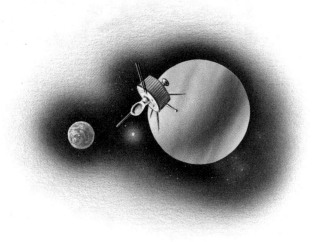

1
Out of This World

Would you like to take the trip of a lifetime?

How about going to an orbiting sports complex where you can participate in a *zero-gravity* (weightless) Olympic Games? Can you imagine taking a field trip to the historic site of the first moon landing? Does visiting a theme park in space or taking a trip to Mars interest you?

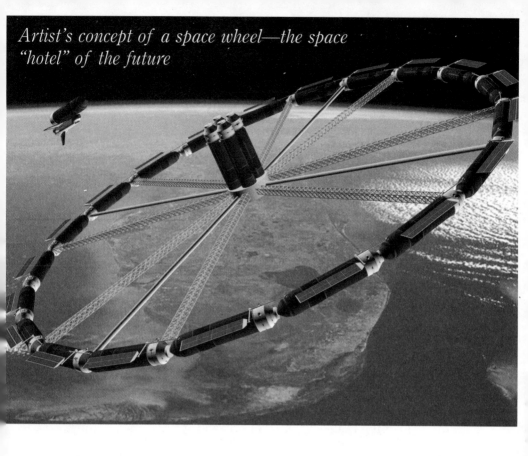

Artist's concept of a space wheel—the space "hotel" of the future

If you said yes to any of these questions, you are ready to be a *space tourist*! People just like you, not only trained astronauts, want the adventure of traveling in space. Companies are planning for space tourism. They are developing new spacecrafts. They are designing plans for towns on the moon with parks and special attractions, and even floating space hotels.

Don't worry if you miss your space shuttle flight to your space hotel. Just hop aboard the nearest space elevator! Press the button for the top floor. The magnetized vehicle you are riding in will climb a *very* long cable. The plans for this awesome elevator are being developed right now.

NASA's model of a space elevator

Stop by your space hotel, but don't be surprised if there is no bed for you—or for *anybody*! Instead, strap yourself into a sleeping bag that is attached to a support pad. Then clip the pad to the inside of a sleep bunk so you don't float away or bump into anybody or anything because of weightlessness.

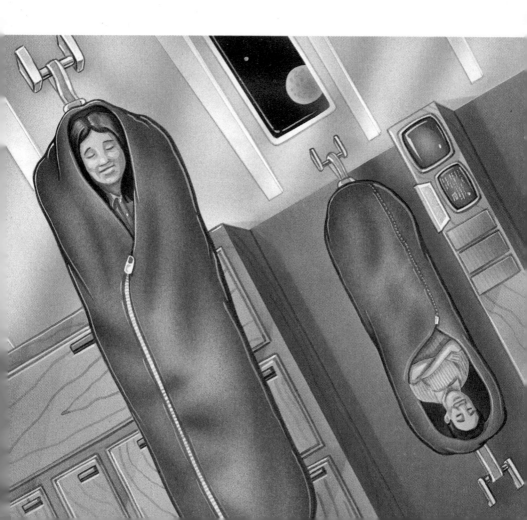

This is one way the astronauts and cosmonauts who are working and living in space at the ISS (International Space Station) sleep. The ISS is a huge orbiting laboratory that helps scientists learn more about space. At the ISS, the crew learns how people can live in space for future explorations. But to truly understand the future of space exploration, it is important to look back . . . sometimes *way* back.

2

Cool Space People

Around 3000 BC, the ancient Babylonians studied the skies. They lived in what is present-day Iraq. They were among the earliest astronomers. Astronomers are scientists who study objects in space. They identified constellations, or groupings of stars, as seen from Earth. They made charts of the stars they saw.

The Chinese, around 2500 BC, began to observe planets and developed a 365-day calendar. They based the calendar on the belief that the sun took 365 days to journey across the sky.

It is believed that some of the ancient pyramids in Egypt, including the Great Pyramid (built around 2700 BC), point to a certain constellation or star. According to this theory, the pyramids were built to help the dead find their way to the afterlife.

The Sun Stone, an Aztec stone calendar

The Mayas, of present-day Central America, and the Aztecs, of present-day central Mexico, also looked to the stars for answers. Like the Chinese, they used the skies to create a calendar. We know this from the buildings and artifacts they left behind.

There are 365 steps on this Mayan pyramid,
the number of days in a solar year.

Ptolemy (TOL-uh-me) (c. AD 120–180) was a Greek astronomer. He is known as the "Father of Astronomy." He believed that Earth was at the center of the universe.

Thirteen centuries later, Nicolaus Copernicus, a Polish lawyer (1473–1543), developed a new theory that put the sun at the center of the universe.

Ptolemy

Nicolaus Copernicus

Galileo Galilei (1564–1642), an Italian astronomer and mathematician, made a telescope and viewed outer space with it. Like Copernicus, he thought the sun was the center of the universe.

Galileo demonstrating his telescope

In England, Isaac Newton (1642–1727) improved upon the telescope. He also developed the theory of *gravity,* the invisible "pulling power" that holds everything on Earth to the ground. Newton applied this same idea of gravity to the sun and planets. Actually, all the objects in the universe—planets, moons, and stars—have gravity, too. It is gravity that keeps them all in line!

3
On Your Mark—
Get Set—Go!

Today many countries work together and share ideas as they explore outer space. That was not always the case. Not too long ago, countries were actually racing to get into space first.

On October 4, 1957, a satellite called *Sputnik I* was launched by the Soviet Union. A satellite is a spacecraft built to orbit, or travel around, Earth or another planet.

This ball-shaped satellite was very tiny but *very* mighty. It only measured 23 inches across but it weighed 184 pounds! It took 90 minutes for it to orbit Earth.

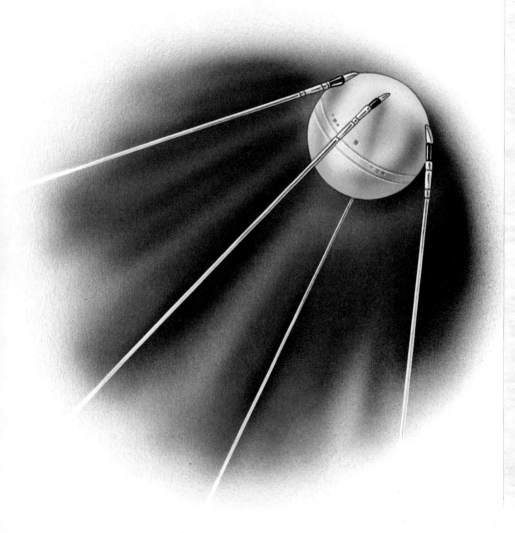

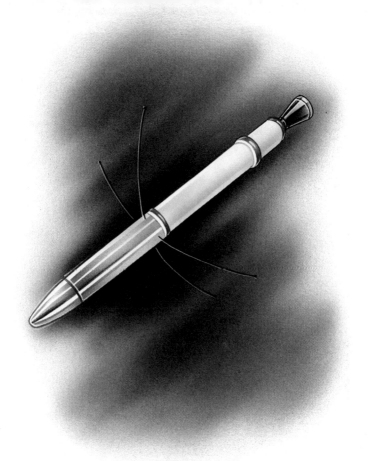

The United States worked fast and hard as well. On January 31, 1958, it launched its first successful satellite— *Explorer I*. But *Sputnik I* beat *Explorer I* into space by 119 days. The space race was on!

Both countries sped toward the next challenge. It was time to see if a living creature could survive traveling in space.

4
Moonwalk Your Dog!

Question: What do dogs, monkeys, rats, mice, fish, ants, spiders, bullfrogs, honey-bees, and jellyfish have in common?
Answer: They all have been travelers in space!

In fact, animals went up in space before the first human did. Scientists wanted to learn how an animal's body could handle space travel. This way, scientists could make sure that space travel would be safe for humans.

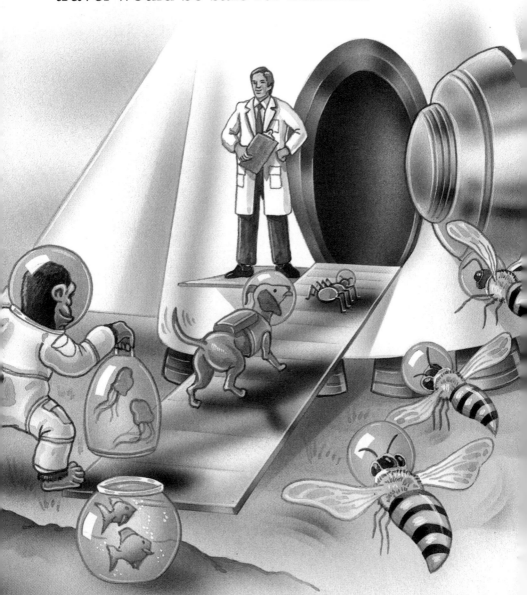

In 1957, the first living creature to travel in space was a dog named Laika (LAY-kuh; "Barker" in English). She traveled in the Soviet spacecraft *Sputnik II*. Sadly, *Sputnik II* was not designed to return safely to Earth. After a week of orbiting in space, Laika died due to lack of air to breathe.

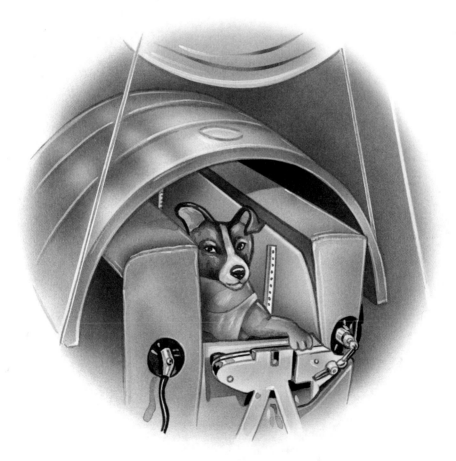

Strelka and Belka

In 1961, the Soviet Union sent up two other dogs, Strelka ("Little Arrow") and Belka ("Squirrel"). They traveled in *Sputnik V*. They orbited Earth for one day. Both dogs returned safely.

Dogs were not the only early space
travelers. Gordo, a squirrel monkey, was
the first monkey to go up in space. He took
his trip in 1958 aboard the Jupiter AM-13
missile. Everything went well in flight.
After the return trip, the rocket landed in
the water as planned. But a flotation
device did not work. Gordo was lost at sea.

Ham, a chimpanzee, trained for more than a year before he was sent into space. He learned to pull a right-hand lever when a white light flashed and to pull a left-hand lever when a blue light flashed. He was rewarded with banana pellets, which made his training very "appealing"! In 1961, this astrochimp made his safe flight on the Mercury Redstone 2 rocket.

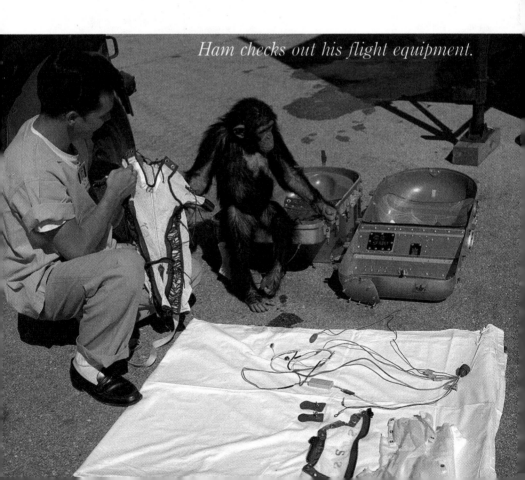

Ham checks out his flight equipment.

All of the animal space explorers paved the way for space travel by humans. Here are a few space pioneers who paved the way for others:

COOL SPACE TRAVELERS

 **Yuri Gagarin** was the first person in space and first to orbit Earth on April 12, 1961.

Alan Shepard was the first American in space on May 5, 1961.

John Glenn was the first American to orbit Earth on February 20, 1962.

Valentina Tereshkova (vah-layn-TEE-nuh tuh-resh-KOH-vuh) was the first woman to travel into space on June 16, 1963.

Sally Ride was the first American woman in space on June 18, 1983.

Neil Armstrong was the first person to walk on the moon on July 20, 1969.

Guion "Guy" Bluford was the first African American in space on August 30, 1983.

Mae C. Jemison was the first African American woman in space on September 12, 1992.

Ellison Onizuka was the first Asian American in space on January 24, 1985. He was killed in the explosion of the space shuttle *Challenger* on January 28, 1986.

Franklin Chang-Diaz was the first Hispanic in space on January 12, 1986.

Ellen Ochoa was the first Hispanic woman in space on April 4, 1993.

5

Space Wanderers

As a future space tourist, you have something in common with the planets. The word "planet" comes from a Greek word that means "wanderer." One day you may wander the solar system, and possibly beyond into the universe. But first it might help to know the places you will see on your travels.

The solar system is centered around
the sun. All of the objects in the system,
from a tiny bit of dust to the most faraway
planet, orbit and spin around the sun.

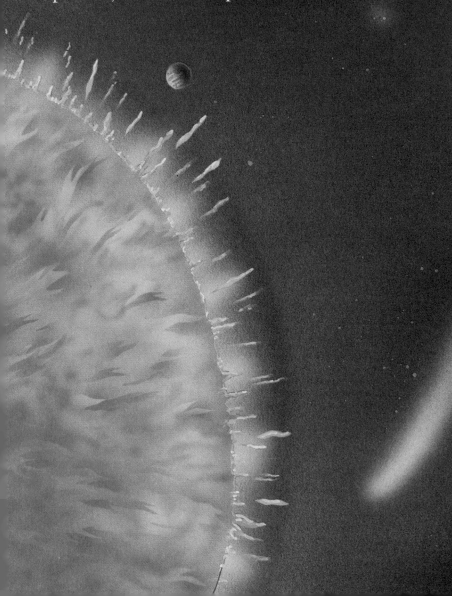

After all, the word "solar" means "of the sun." It is the sun's gravity that locks all of its orbiting objects into place.

The sun is a star. Like all stars, it is
a huge ball of exploding, hot gases. It is
close enough to Earth for us to benefit
from its light and heat. The sun is a
medium-sized star with a diameter about
109 times more than that of Earth. There
are at least 100 billion stars in our galaxy,
the Milky Way. A galaxy is a grouping of
stars, and the sun is just one of the group.

A planet is an enormous round object made up of rock or gas. It orbits and spins around the sun. It does not make its own light. Planets reflect the light of the sun. The nine planets in our solar system (in order of closeness to the sun) are: Mercury, Venus, Earth, Mars, Jupiter, Saturn, Uranus, Neptune, and Pluto.

A photo of Saturn and its ring system

All of the planets, except Mercury and Venus, have moons that orbit around them. Four of the planets, Jupiter, Saturn, Uranus, and Neptune, have a system of rings around them. The rings may look solid, but they are actually made up of separate ice-covered rocks. The rocks range in size from dust-sized specks to rocks as big as mountains. The brightest rings belong to Saturn.

Artist's concept of Sedna—a possible planet on the outer edge of the solar system

Some astronomers think there might actually be more planets in our solar system. And some astronomers believe that frosty Pluto is not a planet at all. There is an icy cluster of objects just past Neptune, and Pluto is the largest one.

And those are the cold, hard (and sometimes hot) facts about our solar system!

A photo of Pluto taken by the Hubble Space Telescope

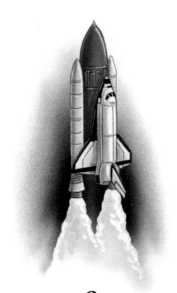

6

Get Ready to Go

Now that you know what is in the solar
system, you are ready to plan your trip.
Do you have an extra 20 million dollars?
That's what it cost California businessman
Dennis Tito to buy a "ticket" to be the first
space tourist. He was launched into space
on April 28, 2001, in the Russian *Soyuz*
capsule and spent six days on the ISS!

Hopefully, the price will come *way* down when it's your turn to be a space tourist so you'll have a little money left over to buy some space souvenirs!

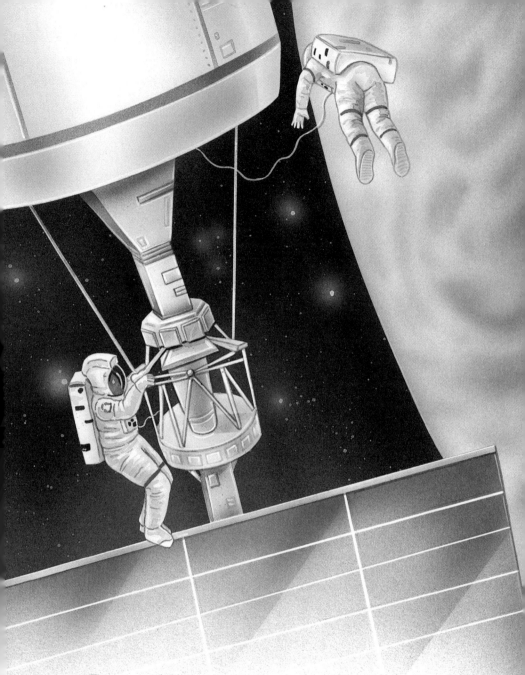

Remember to study your Russian,
Italian, and French. These are just a few of
the languages that are spoken on the ISS.

The United States and Russia are working together, along with 14 other countries, to make the ISS a success. It is being built in space, piece by piece. When it's finished, the ISS will be equal to the size of about two football fields. It is so heavy that it can only be built in the weightlessness of space. Upon its completion in 2006, 43 shuttle trips to the ISS will have brought up all the different equipment and parts that it's made up of.

Artist's concept of the International Space Station

*Two astronauts at work on
the Hubble Space Telescope*

While you are packing, check to see that your camera works, too! In 1990, astronauts on the space shuttle *Discovery* launched the first orbiting space telescope—the Hubble Space Telescope. This telescope was sent into outer space to give scientists a closer look at the universe. At first, the Hubble was sending back pictures that were out of focus because the lens was bad! In 1993, astronauts from the space shuttle *Endeavor* did some spacewalking and repaired it.

Hubble pictures before the lens was repaired . . . and after

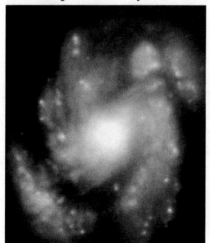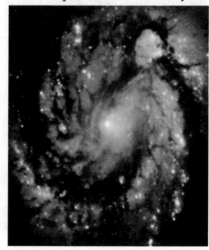

More photos from the Hubble Space Telescope

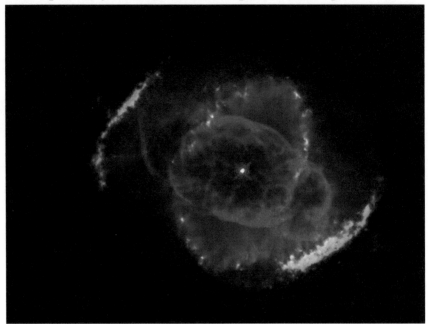

Cat's Eye Nebula

Sombrero Nebula

Yuri Malenchenko (left), the cosmonaut who got married while on the ISS, with American astronaut Ed Lu

Outer space is a great place to have a party. Already there has been the first space wedding. On August 10, 2003, Russian cosmonaut Yuri Malenchenko married Ekaterina Dmitriev. Yuri was living aboard the ISS at the time, but the wedding took place at the Johnson Space Center in Houston, Texas, via video. During the party, Ekaterina stood next to a life-sized cutout of Yuri.

Hopefully, all your friends can make
the trip to *your* out-of-this-world party.
Anything is possible in space!
Enjoy the trip!
(And don't forget your toothbrush!)